IMPOSSIBLE MEMORIES

CHRIS TUTTON

AVALANCHE BOOKS

Published in Great Britain by Avalanche Books, England 2016

Printed by SRP

British Library Cataloguing in Publication Data. A catalogue record for this book is available from the British Library.

ISBN: 978 1 874392 22 4

By the same author:

Ariadne's Lament (1993)
Acnestis in Elysium (1995)
Ecumenical Shadows (1998)
Rain Angel (2003)
Seasons of Winter (2005)
Angles of Repose (2012)

Pendulum (2008)
Of Love and Hope (2010)
Seductive Harmonies (2012)
Wordstrokes (2015)

CONTENTS

**IN THE BEGINNING WE REFUSED
TO BELIEVE THAT OLD AGE
WOULD NOT ANNOUNCE ITSELF
UPON ITS ARRIVAL, BUT IT HAD
BEEN A GUEST IN OUR HOUSE
LONG BEFORE EITHER OF US
REALISED THAT IT WAS THERE.
WE EXCUSED IT TO OUR FRIENDS
AND MADE ALLOWANCES FOR ITS
GAUCHE MANNERISMS, BUT IT
TOOK INCREASING EXCEPTION
TO WHAT IT CONSIDERED TO
BE OUR PATRONISING ATTITUDE
AND THREATENED TO KILL US**

It was only between our little
moments of uncertainty that

we became aware that there
were greater things to be

unsure of.

A MOMENTARY EPOCH OF APPREHENSION

He bows into your gaze
a little cautious of your

eye. The butterfly wing
of your passing cheek

just close enough to be
crushed by a footstep.

A PASSIONATE CONFLICT OF CONVICTIONS

Was it true for you that the
maimed were best practiced

in the arts of love?

Or was truth a necessary delusion?
because like all the other women of

Themiscyra, you

held your breast so much
cheaper than war.

A PRAYER FOR THE DAMNED

If I was young and strong
enough

to reach inside this
bygone book of sleep,

I'd sweep my brabbled
memories clean and

trade with such exquisite
dreams

these flotsam days of
careworn wanderings.

A TENTATIVE SUPPLICATION

The curious thing about your faith

is

how you insinuate your devotion;

surreptitiously

rubbing your hands together in prayer

as if warming them from the cold.

AN AGE OF REMEMBRANCE

In the monastery of your arms rests a
lawn of braille where I garden sleep,

by the millhouse of your summer lips
and the breath of your slumber song,

beneath the open parasol of your kiss,
among downy-soft hatchling mornings

where we seeded ourselves meadows of
wilder flowers; you, musk mallow pink,

shimmering down to the river
in a cloud of wings.

AN UNEXPECTED CHRISTMAS PRESENT AND THE CONSEQUENT DAWN OF A BEAUTIFUL NEW FRIENDSHIP

But for an innocent
slip of the tongue

you may only ever
have given me socks.

ASPHODEL

With the liniment of this
brush I could raise you to

the carnival of your colour,
steal you from nothingness,

reach inside your garden and
throw petals of daylight onto

your sleep; dream your little
scalloped eyelids open with a kiss.

A VERY NEARLY INADVERTENTLY UNREQUITED FULL THREE ACTS OF CALAMITOUS RECONCILIATION

In the quietus of this night we must
forsake our yield. Surrender our
turning leaves to the wind. You will

squeeze my hand gently with your far-
away eyes, sing something sotto voce,
sweet, warm as a tear. And I will need to

find myself among you somewhere;
angle my deafness towards the trailing inky
nimbus of your verse, just far enough

away from its sleepless thunder to
hear you breathe, sail over the shifting
sands of my incurably inconsonant reply.

FAWNING IN LOVE AGAIN

Your wool is coarse as a
drunken curse, yet I wear it

next to my skin; keeps me
standing here at the font of

the brook, tending another
absent flock in the rain.

FROM THE NIGHT GARDEN

We were only ever
children of the old;

soft as wishes, swollen-
bellied, thirsty for

songs of the rain.
We lingered there

until the river had
spoken; your kisses

growing hard and
sinewy as the wind.

I MERELY SUGGESTED
THAT BEFORE YOU
ATTEMPTED TO
TAKE THE SPLINTER
OUT OF MY EYE YOU
SHOULD REMOVE
THE PLANK FROM
YOUR OWN.
THIS YOU PROMPTLY
DID AND RUTHLESSLY
BLUDGEONED ME INTO
SUBMISSION WITH IT

I lost you in the quick-
sand of words by the

amusement arcade
on the old pier of

pretending that
neither of us would ever

leave the other alone to
take

so readily to the sea.

A FRAGMENT OF TOUCH

Toy piano drizzles into
a plaintive mist of you;

becomes the

long, warm grass of a
time when I held you in

my breath,

and diligently dressed
such brittle notes

in feelings.

I TOOK YOU TO THE MOST ROMANTIC SUBTEXT IN THE WORLD AND YOU DIDN'T EVEN RECOGNISE THE LANDMARKS

Maybe I should have held you a little tighter
in the slip joint pliers of my palm when I
pulled you like a tooth into the mullioned rain.

Dried you off, rubbed you down, dubbed you
Odile and ran through the evening pristine
pearly limbs of the Louvre with you warm and

young. Maybe I could have confessed something
kind, cinematic, technicolour; staffed the talkie of
your ear when it turned silent against me, ghostly,

monochrome, menacingly moonlit; followed the
fuming steam of your breathless express past the
polyphonic choral evensong sots staggering like

sidemen to the wind, overblowing offbeat
cooler than cold all the way down the ineffable
burden of the Boulevard Saint-Michel.

PALIMPSEST

We break into weeping candlelight,
snatch blindly at shadows; fall as
petals in the flicker. Contract, vanish

entwined into the crematory soot of our
corpora. Become cinders of touch,
the smoky catacomb walls of our words,

acrid elegies for flesh.

A PEACE SO CLOSE TO COMFORT

Somewhere above the stave, the double-
dogged Golgotha of that day, adrift,

unanchored from his brood, his
black eye turned inward to nest amid

the sweeping reach of her tree;

his soft sleep weightless upon
her kiss, his broken brushes, her

fresh green leaves stuffed like nails
into the thinning branches

of his sky.

THE ARCHER

Then, when the day has broken,
I will sit beside myself and

gather pieces of you on the
mossy bevel of the Lethe; polish

them up a little with my long-ago,
soft and sleepless eyes, love and

kiss them tenderly, ordain them
each and always summer; bind them

together with the unflowering twine of
my keep and aim them dearly

sorrowful as an arrow at the sun;
and know as I have always known

that they will surely ride the wind
when my selfbow creaks and breaks.

THE RESISTANCE OF MEMORY

We could live so well then,
in the cavernous emptiness of
each other's words; spend

idyllic holidays beached on
subterfuge, wade out of
our depth in clear blue water.

We could render the render of
our evenings nourishing then,
perch at the edge of the surf and

watch our reflections in the polished
half-full glass of things we hadn't said,
hardly finding words to notice

how the torch light dying lay
strewn around us like summers
buttoned up to the chin.

THE LONG DRIFT BACK TO THE SKY

In the amber of the hour
pearly curtains fly half-mast on
a shallow sigh of autumn. The

wax moon of your cheekbone
yellows.

In weeping gardens we
peck like sparrows at
the crumbs of your breath;

drown and weave on the
tidal reaches of your little waves;

ride the midnight ferry of your fingers
into a drift of retreat, wait
like curious children to remember a

golden sunrise in this crowning
Season of Forgetfulness.

THE BIRTH OF OCEANS

We huddle abreast in the
gospel of our

desolute sunset.

Quantify our solitude
with a different tongue.

In the morning
we will no longer

be young.

Together we will
shoulder the loneliness

of being together.

THE HOME OF THE MUSES

...and after your hair had tumbled down the
dreams of Mount Parnassus like a flock of

uncounted sheep, turning the
pheasant's-eye green, gathering

orchids to spread like a mossy cradle onto
my misty eyes sleepy with wine, it became

a squall of impossible memories, taking to
muscari milky blue skies above the olive groves

like a tangle of ravens.

THE LOOP ROUTE

By vespers we had side-stepped the
doormat dead, danced lazily, dreamy

among the pipistrelles. Following the

slithering sundown of our aimless amble,
the rowdy home-crowd chants of bush-

crickets in the after dinner grass raised our

floundering game to wish the long night
light enough to see that all we really wanted

was to settle seamlessly into each other and

live weightless above the graveyard
for an hour.

THE MYTH OF EDEN

You have merited your madness
through chastening pains, in blistering
summer fields of reason, winters
of love. You have borne him the

sick child of your hunger, watched
the fruit of your altar moulder and
frost; the furnace of your nakedness
not even ripening the apple of his hand.

THE SPIRAL PAINTER

Now I wait for you in altered oils,
framed, unframed, a little dark and
rubbed around the edges; dressed,

undressed, I caress you with the
edge of my finger.

Now I animate you in arcadian reflections;
colour still holds me,
neither of us is lost.

Now I retouch everything. The stammer, the
sough, the bits no-one else can see; beyond the
yellow varnish of the horizon, the impossible sky.

THE TRANSIENCE OF ETERNAL LOVE

What matters is the
way you

touch my hand

when you tell me
how

Iliona seized Polymestor's eyes;

sinking your fingernails
further and

further into my flesh,

as if to motion the
reassurance

that you could

never be so moved
to hurt me.

THE PIPER

I will inflate you with the
fiery bellows of my sorrow,

gild you with the intangible
gold of dreams; play you

over and over as you recede
note by note into distance;

release you blackly from the
racked clutch of my kiss; your

broken child, the garden of
your cheek, the holy water

of your hand, ink on my pages.

SCHRODINGER'S CATASTROPHE: THE PERSISTENCE OF DILEMMA

This perpetual agony of
breath somehow always

compels me to breathe.

Such insistence on
belief leaves me

broken with desire.

My untamed aversion to
knowing curses me over and

over with the possibility that

even you could always soon
be light enough to be warm.

THREE HAIKU
(MINUS TWO)

When she touches him
he will almost remember
the weight of his hands.

WHILE OLD MEN BATHED IN RIVERS OF RAIN

We gathered wool
from the spineless

barbs of invisible
fences, which had

only recently been
re-erected to remind

us that the sheep had
sneaked in and stolen

all our coats that we had
collected so meticulously

for the winter.

THE PERFIDIOUS LEGACY OF ILLUSION

You remain as a virus in
my lifeforce; floating around,

a fetid foetus in the darkwater.

Pissing in the soup of my
memory, decanting my best

Burmese ruby blood into the

sick-bag of your sap, heaping
straw upon straw, breaking in

the bark of the bletcherous
dog-in-the-manger day beside you.

A DISQUIETING SILENCE

It was the acrid stew of rotting rats and blossoming damp
which hacked the back of the throat like a razor in the
inner porch of the corpse that had once been a home.
There was nothing else left in it now. Just wind and
bones.
She was a woman. She had wanted to be adored. She had
needed at least to be loved. She fixed her face in the scar
of a mirror, twisted the rope of her auburn hair around a
pin and left her life bit by bit through a crack of muffled
street light falling like roadkill around the peeling frame
of her back door.
It was raining. More in than out. Unfingered by sirens
she slinked hooded into the trickle, dodging the
headlight-flaming puddles, crossing the road to the
gallows of the night like a cat.
The compulsion to touch something unfamiliar groaned
like a puny-pelvised pre-pubescent giving birth to
nightmare years of unalterable disaffection. She petted a
fleeting memory of a face she had kissed; pressed it
gently with her wet hair. Wished she could kiss it again.
Pushed herself away sharply before she could be burned
by the nearness of it. No-one had noticed the encounter.
She smelled her fingers discretely.
'Nice night for it,' some wire-haired crone wittered
convulsively as they rubbed cliches in neon roselight
outside a brief need to validate something meaningless.
'Yeah, it's worse than ever.'

It was always worse than ever. She could fire it off without even thinking about it. She could slash her wrists with an impromptu exhibition of unguarded humanity and it would never be as bad as this.
Jesus, this was agony. Where the hell were the sirens? She stepped out of the chorus line and into the impending cacophony of disembodied braying seeping through lace-curtained windows, slid her hand between the painted thighs of the glass door and edged her way in.
Inside was like daylight, only worse. Shot, counter-shot, close-up, take, re-take. Uncut footage piled up from the floor to the necks of drunken buccaneers like vomit. A few feet tapped in a breeze of broken tones like gently swaying nooses. If there was a reason to give a damn about what the jukebox was playing it eluded her. She elbowed her way to the bar and waited.
She was breathing hard still, like when he punched her, or kicked her, or forced his hand over her mouth so she couldn't scream. The throb in the billowing volume of squeals became a heartbeat. She squeezed herself into a tiny space between the sudden chinks of glasses. The rats will have found him by now. Will have started poking around in his face. She wiped her trembling hands in her skirt for the umpteenth time. Partially hidden by a backstage babbling barbershop quartet of pirouetting Romeos a smiling young girl wore ribbons in her hair.

THE SOCRATIC METHOD

I optimistically proposed that the
apparently unbridgeable gulf between

our problematic perspectives was simply
an awkwardly unanswered question of

dialectics. Your diversivolent
eyebrow briefly considered my

hopeful hypothesis, then dismissively
informed me that I was wrong.

THE GHOST DANCE

In the morning I folded you onto my
pillow, whisper-kissed your blush skin

soft, burrowed for rhymes in the oasis of
your hair, remembered when it was easy,

like listening to Sidney Bechet in the
summer afternoon sun of your fingers.

A MOMENT OF MURMURATION

It took a cyclone of stubborn swallows to
fashion summer from a jumble of rain;

uncouple us from our resinous beds of
reed. Above the clouds we grew feathers

of wind; tumbling and soaring into each
other's drift like a storm of birdsong.

HAIKU FOR YOU
(PLUS TWO)

Your soft eyes fold closed
against the scintillant night;
sorrow bleeds through them.

Wind reads the tall grass,
the page is closed to the sun;
somewhere a plot hides.

You sleep with your back
to the wall of your darkness.
At dawn you will dream.

YOU WHISPERED SWEET NOTHINGS INTO MY EAR WHICH DID NOT AMOUNT TO ANYTHING, BECAME PENITENT AND APPEALED FOR UNDERSTANDING AND COMPASSION. I REASSURED YOU WITH ALL THE FUTILITY OF A PYRRHIC PROMISE THAT DESPITE YOUR BRUTAL HISTORY OF WAR CRIMES I HAD NO WISH TO HANG YOU

You offered me your portrait,
but I had covered my walls

with quadrupeds. Characteristically

undeterred, you became
green again,

an open landscape
untrodden by sheep.

SOMETIMES THERE WERE TIMES WHEN THE TIMES THEMSELVES SEEMED TIMELESS

and we wish we had
snatched them up now as
anxious mothers, held
them like sweet secrets,
needled the ink of them into
our skin; wish we had not

lowered our eyeline so gullibly,
or heard them slipping
imponderably into the swim,
to drown in icy waters of such
unimaginably distant lands.

CAESAREAN MORNING

And there you were, as if you
had always been. Flawless.

Ingenuous. All rosy pink and
bloody from sleep;

tempestuously torn from the
gaping belly of the night.

INVISIBLE INK

They were somehow overlooked among
the longueur days in your diary; the
foxed fractures of your epicurian airs;

irresolute passages stuck crudely together
with warm, damp spit from sibilant breezes.
Unpunctuated entries. Amorphous even.

Modest eruptions on the thick skin of
your unbending conceit; and there they
remained, unscratched, inconspicuous, an

oceanic convocation of pustule bores, not yet
tidal in their seepage; harvesting the rolling,
rising moisture of their septic mists around your

all-unsated green and vaunting greed; their
irrepressible irruption wending ever onward
into the nakedly unprotected isthmus of your eye.

A PARAMOUR'S TORMENT: BITTER-SWEET MEMORIES OF LOGOPHILIA AND THE DISCONCERTINGLY ADVENTUROUS ART OF DEFINITION

You were always so immaculately
turned out; every syllable of your

hair coiffeured sculpturally into
substance. A ravishing repository for

languishing letters. A femme fatale
fashionably fascinator-featured beauty. How I

would have crossed burning continents for
you; taken you gladly for my own true and

loved you with a lexicographers lips,
if only you had not persisted as

one of those embarrassingly
awkward words that I could

never quite grasp
the meaning of.

LOTTERY FUNDED
Supported using public funding by
ARTS COUNCIL ENGLAND